Sean Kenney

Cool City

Christy Ottaviano Books
Henry Holt and Company
New York

For Audrey

Henry Holt and Company, LLC
Publishers since 1866
175 Fifth Avenue
New York, New York 10010
mackids.com

Henry Holt® is a registered trademark of
Henry Holt and Company, LLC.

Library of Congress Cataloging-in-Publication Data
Kenney, Sean.
Cool city / Sean Kenney. — 1st ed.
p. cm.
"Christy Ottaviano books."
ISBN 978-0-8050-8762-8
1. Miniature cities and towns—Juvenile literature.
2. Architectural models—Juvenile literature.
3. LEGO toys—Juvenile literature. I. Title.
TT178.K44 2011 745.5928—dc22 2010049001

First Edition—2011 / Book design by Elynn Cohen
LEGO bricks were used to create the models for this book.
The models were photographed by John E. Barrett.
Printed in the United States of America by Worzalla,
Stevens Point, Wisconsin

10 9 8 7 6 5 4

Let's build a city!

Town square	4
Things to do	6
Subway station	8
Skyscraper	10
Aerial view	12
Mini metropolis	14
Traffic jam	16
Street furniture	18
Building styles	20
Building some buildings	23
Elevator	26
Shops	28
City plaza	30
About Sean	32

The city is a great place to be!

好好吃
Chinese Food

There are lots of things to see and to do . . .

RESTAURANT
EAT

6

. . . whether you're underground . . .

Street

Entrance

Station

Ticket machines

Turnstiles

Platform

Pipes and gizmos

X15 Main Street

Subway ↓

Subway ↓

. . . or way up high.

Your building will look even taller if you build the upper floors extra short.

Add gargoyles and other cool decorations.

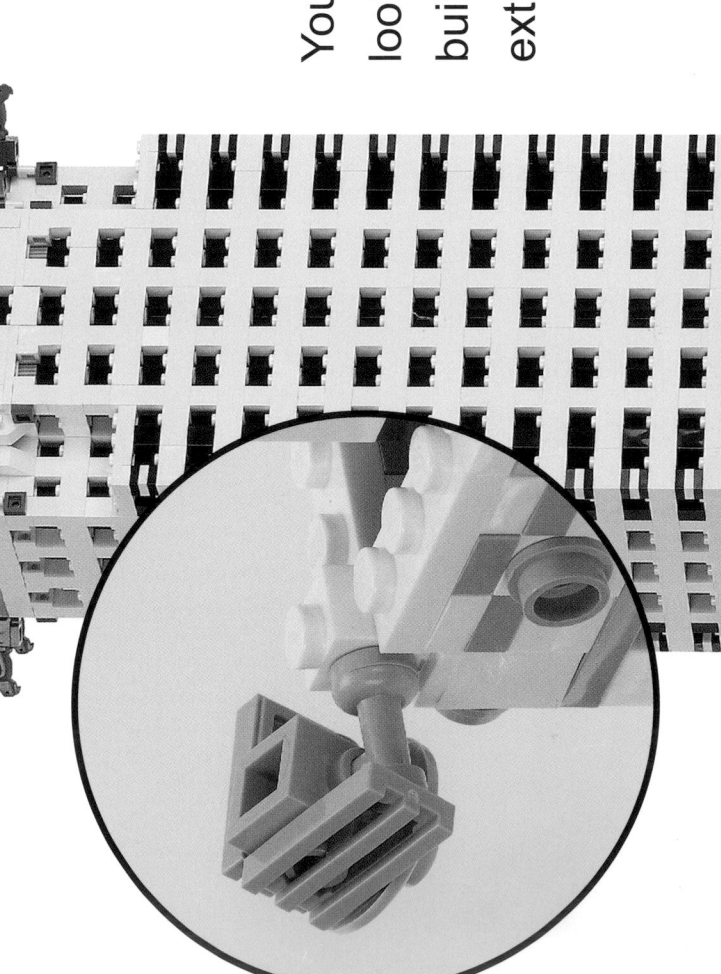

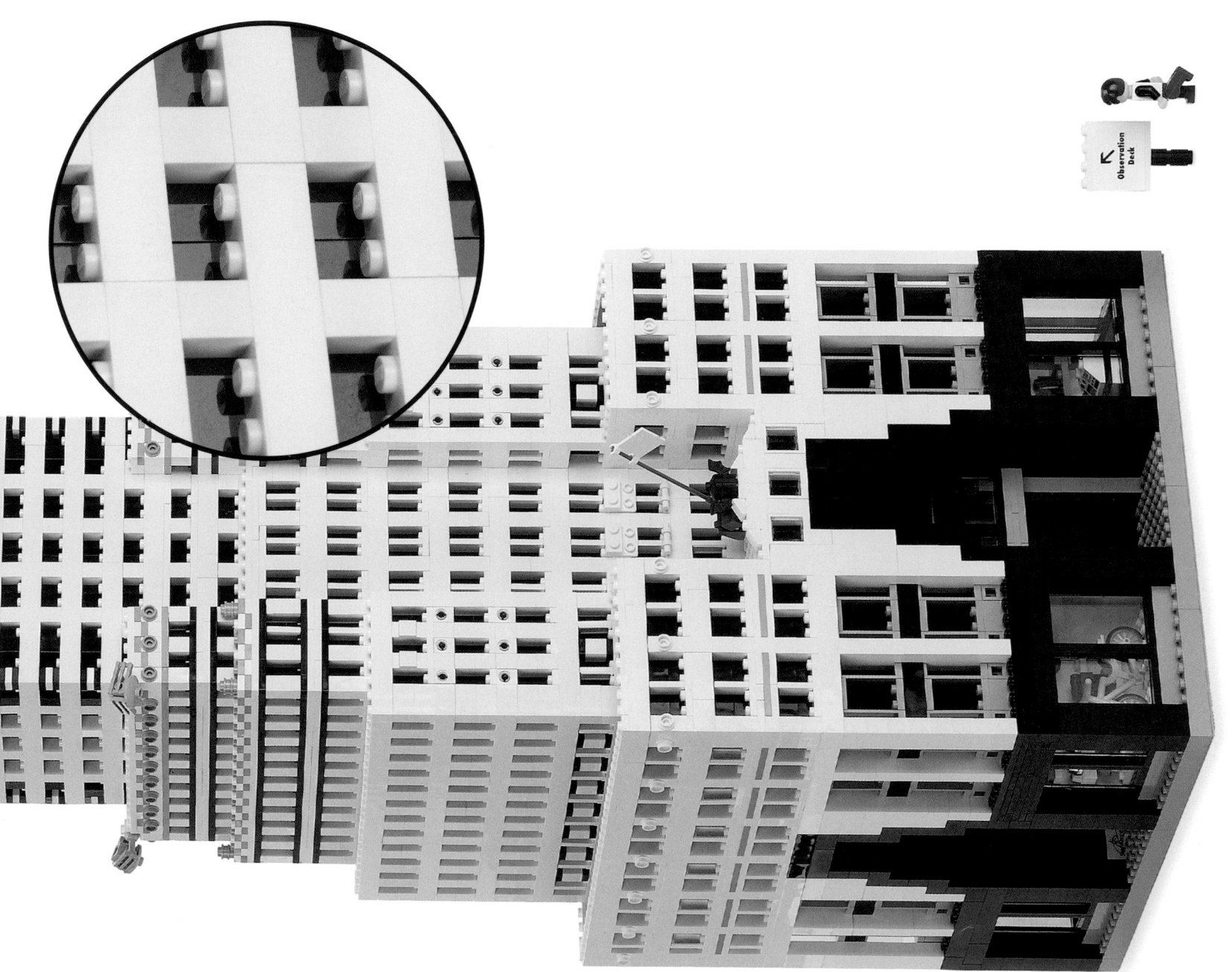

11

What a great view of the city!

13

Make a mini metropolis.

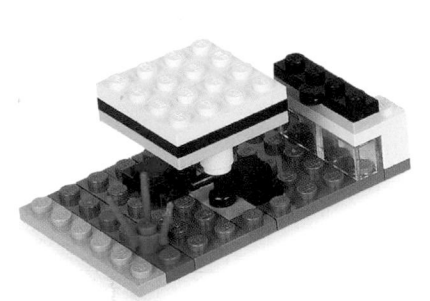

Gas station

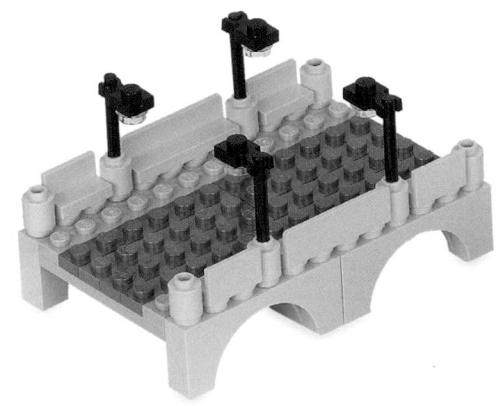

Bridge

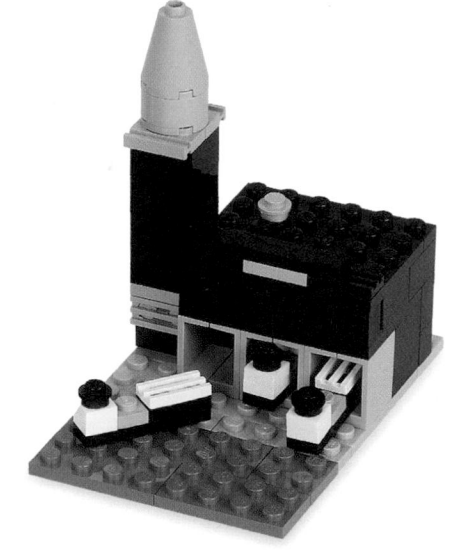

Firehouse

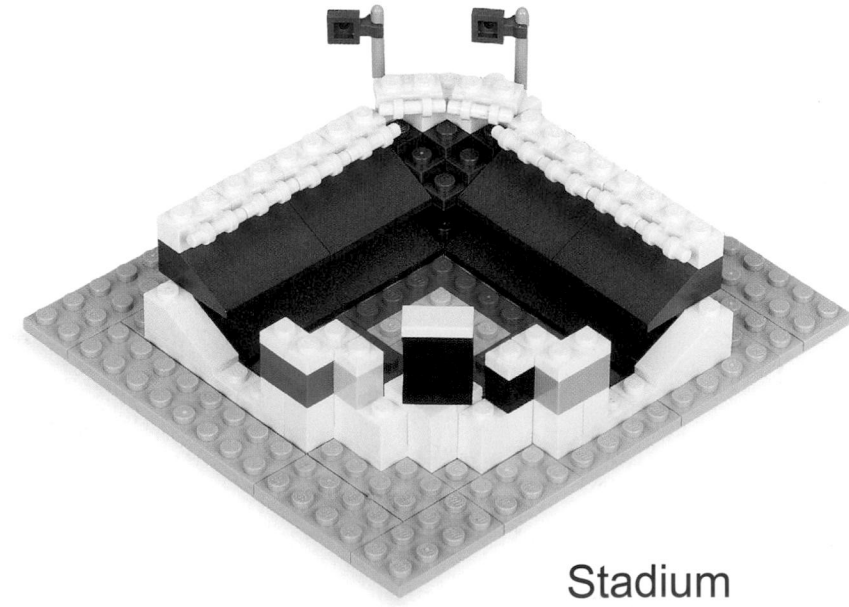

Stadium

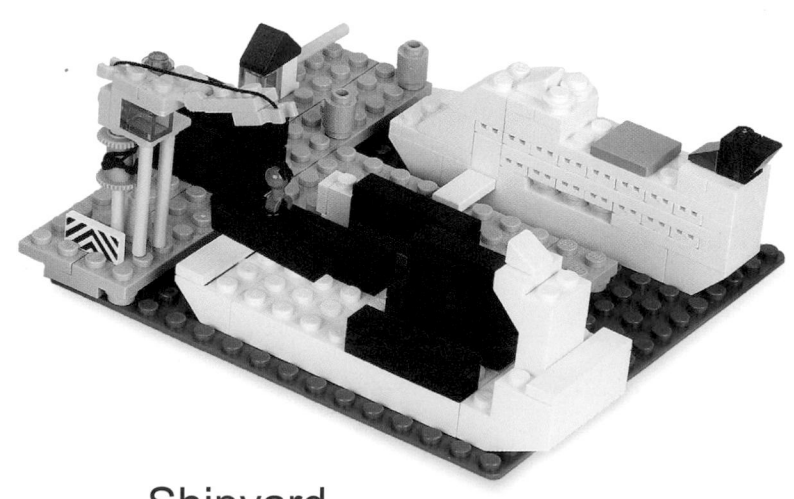

Shipyard

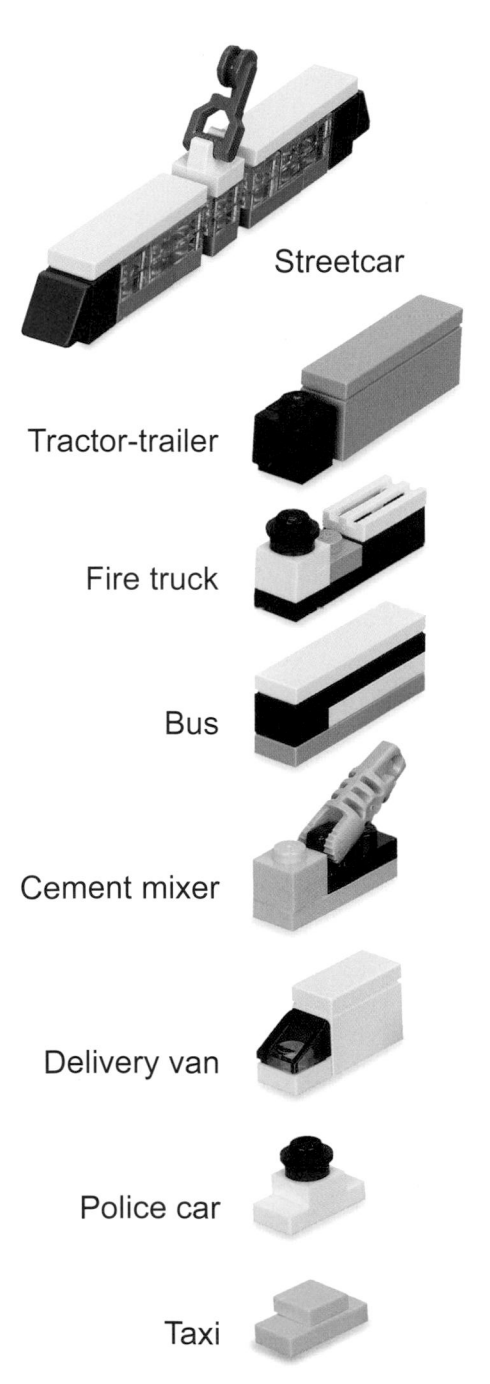

Streetcar

Tractor-trailer

Fire truck

Bus

Cement mixer

Delivery van

Police car

Taxi

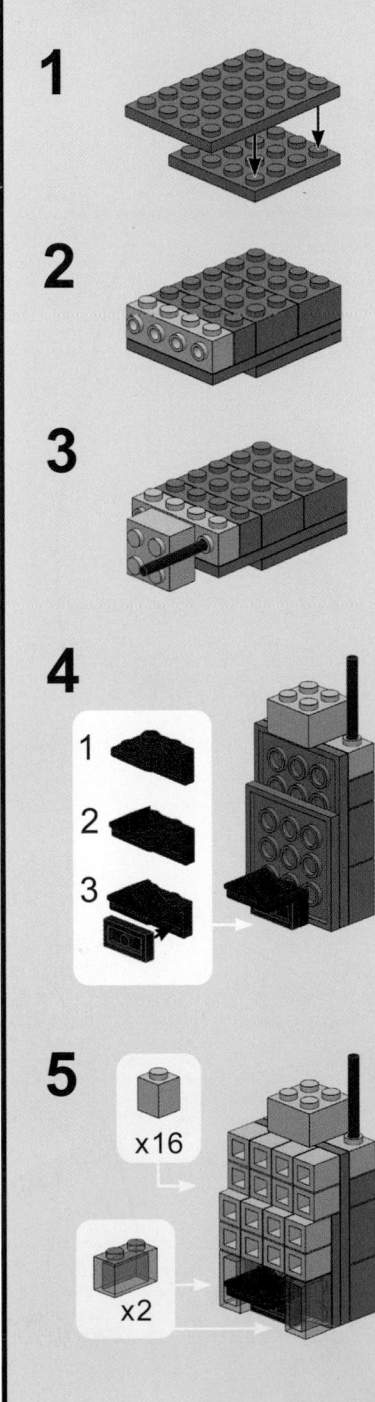

1

2

3

4

1
2
3

5

x16

x2

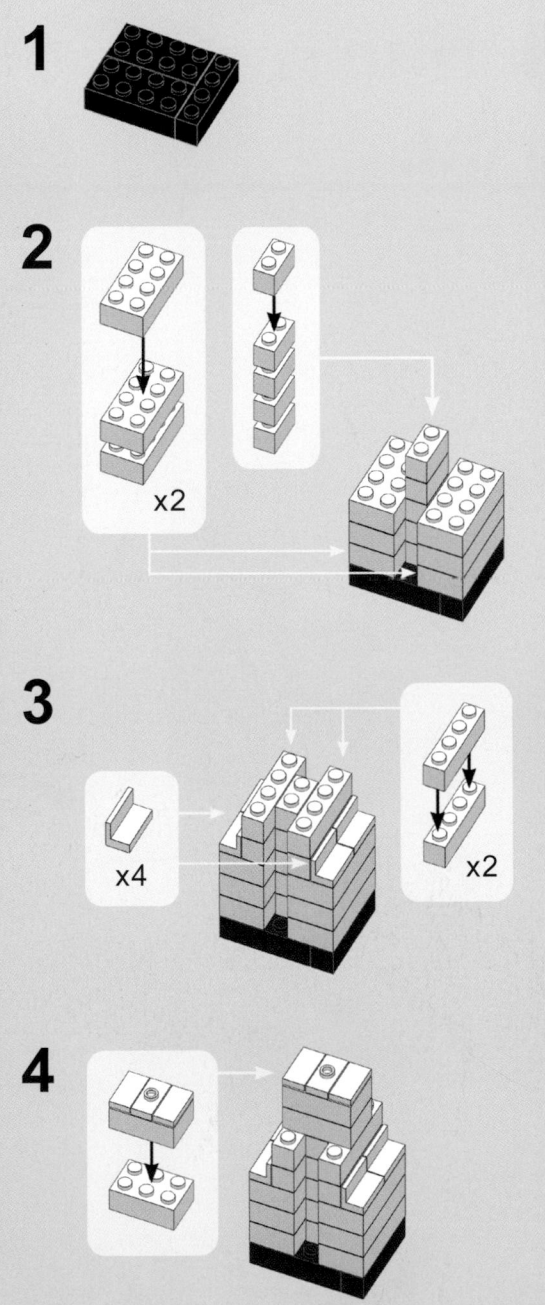

1

2

x2

3

x4

x2

4

5

15

Oh no! Who will fix the traffic jam?

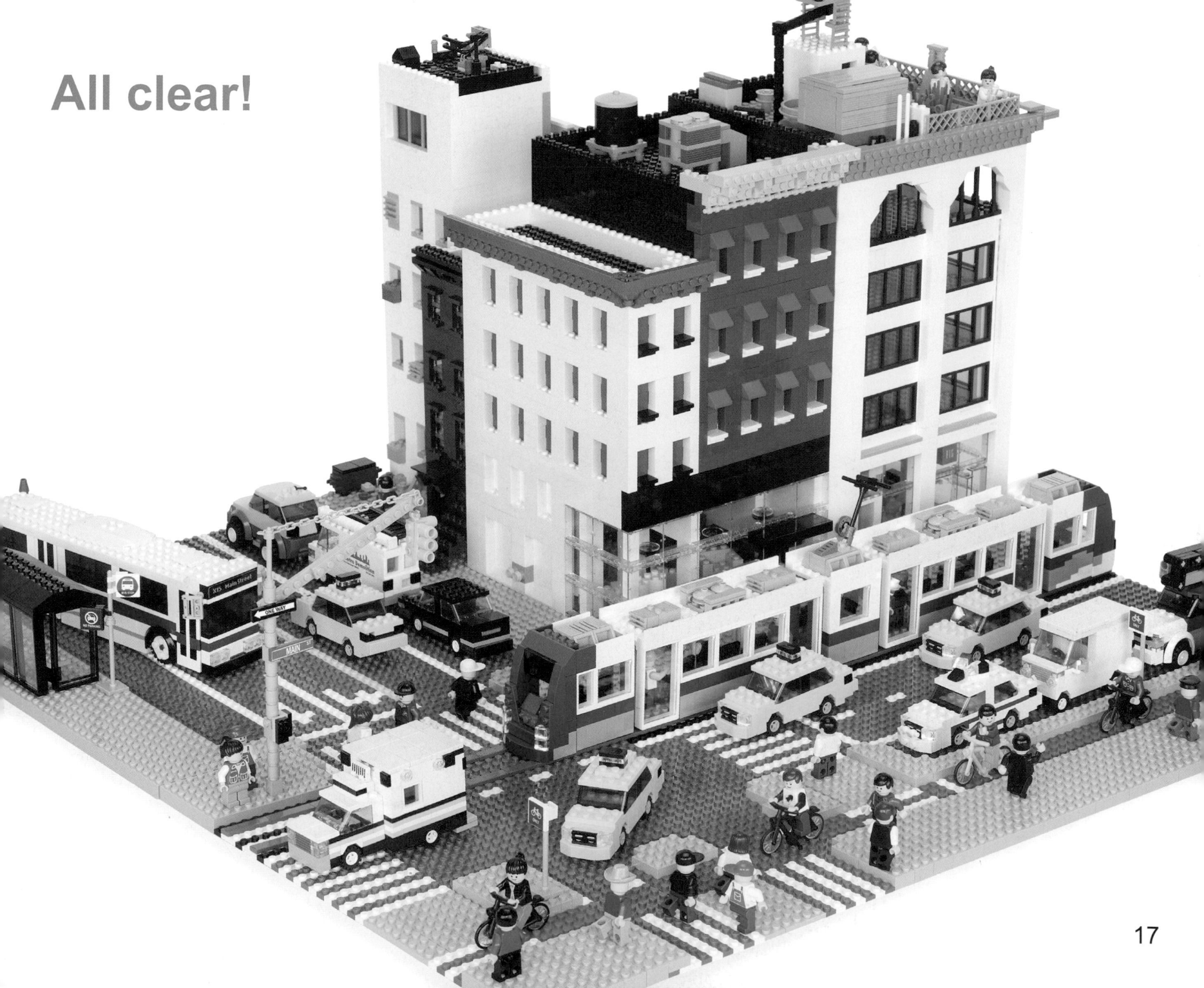

All clear!

Give your street some furniture.

ONE WAY

MAIN ST

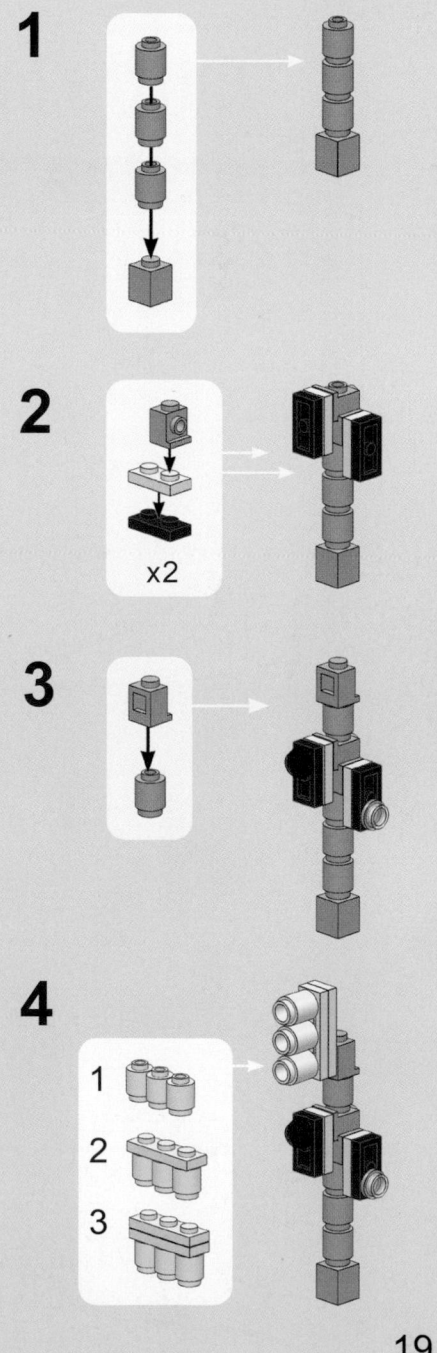

1

2

×2

3

4

1

2

3

19

Different building styles make the city interesting.

New building

Old building

Big building

Small building

Build some buildings

Make your own designs with whatever pieces you have.

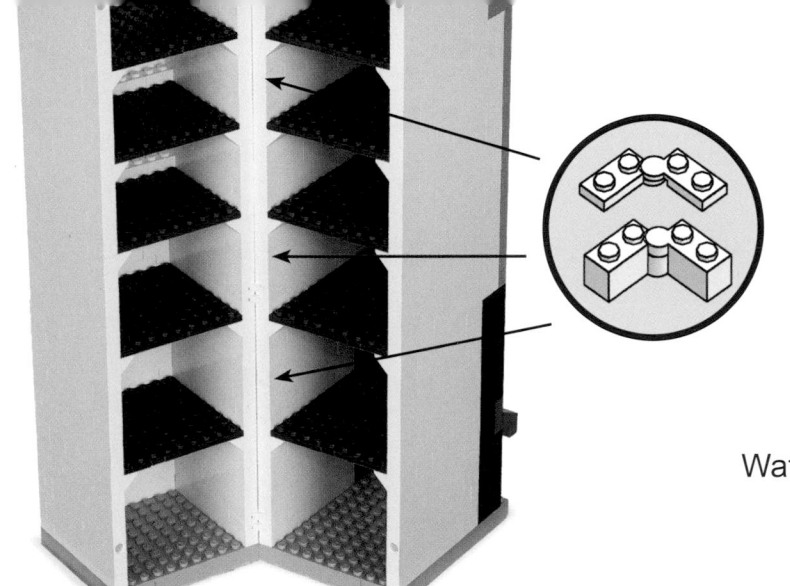

Open the hinges to play inside!

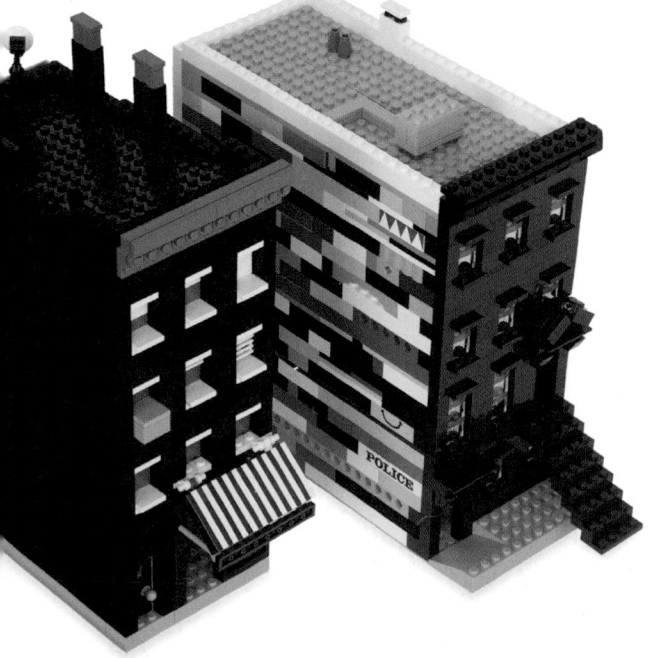

Buildings have lots of cool "roof junk."

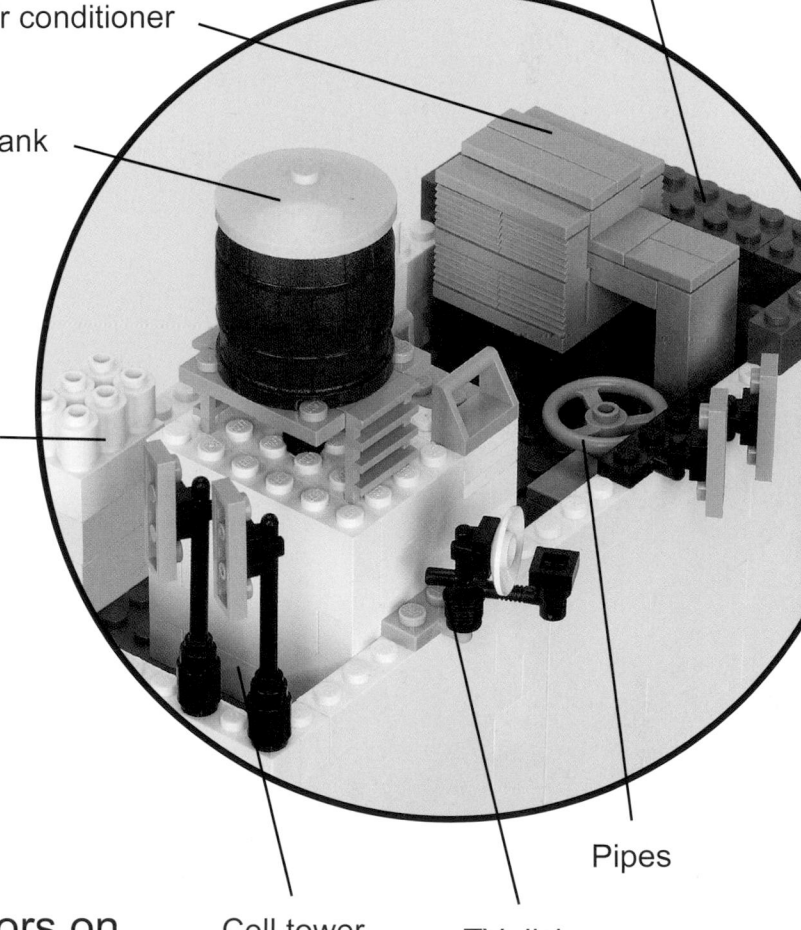

Cornice

Air conditioner

Water tank

Chimney

Cell tower

TV dish

Pipes

Use your extra colors on walls you won't see.

Make a home on Main Street.

1

2

3

4

5

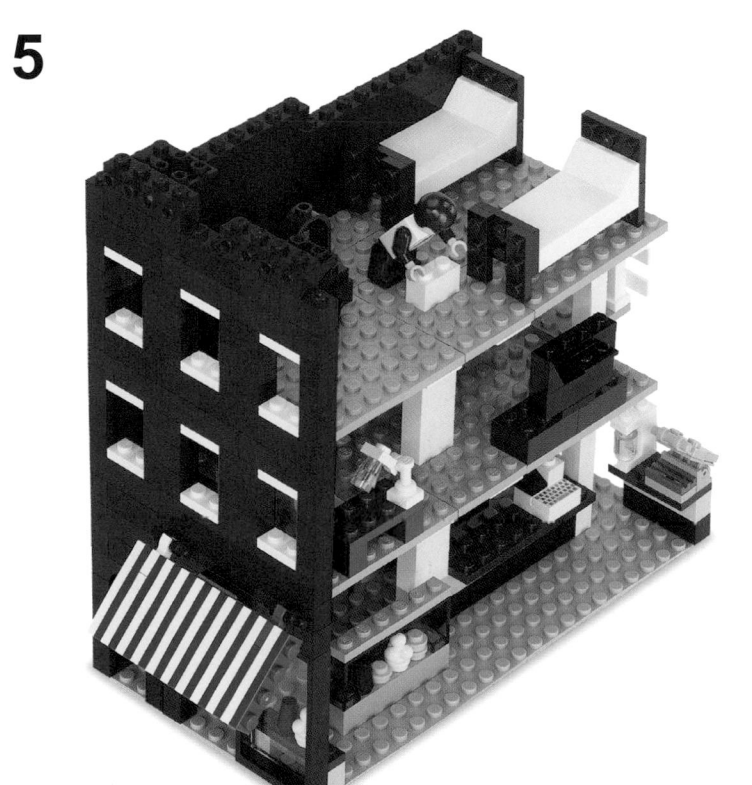

6

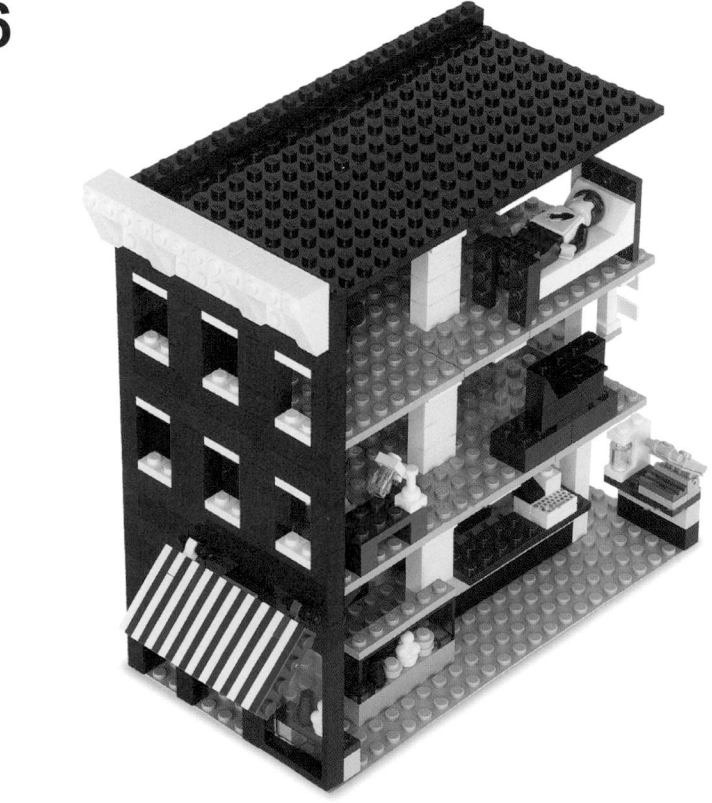

Ride the elevator and visit a home in the sky!

Use a pulley to make your elevator actually work.

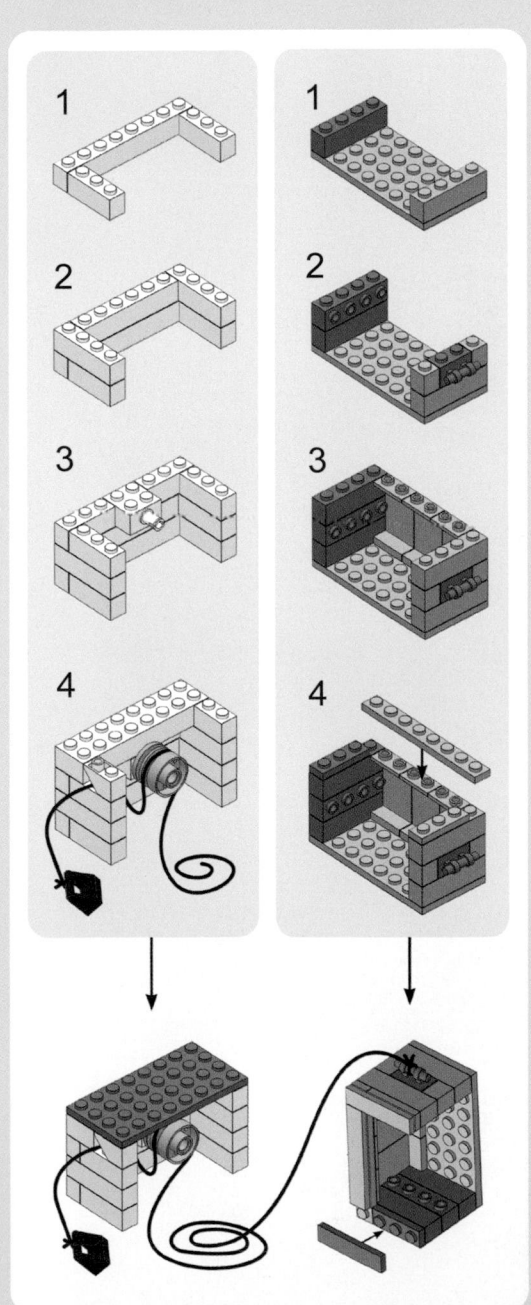

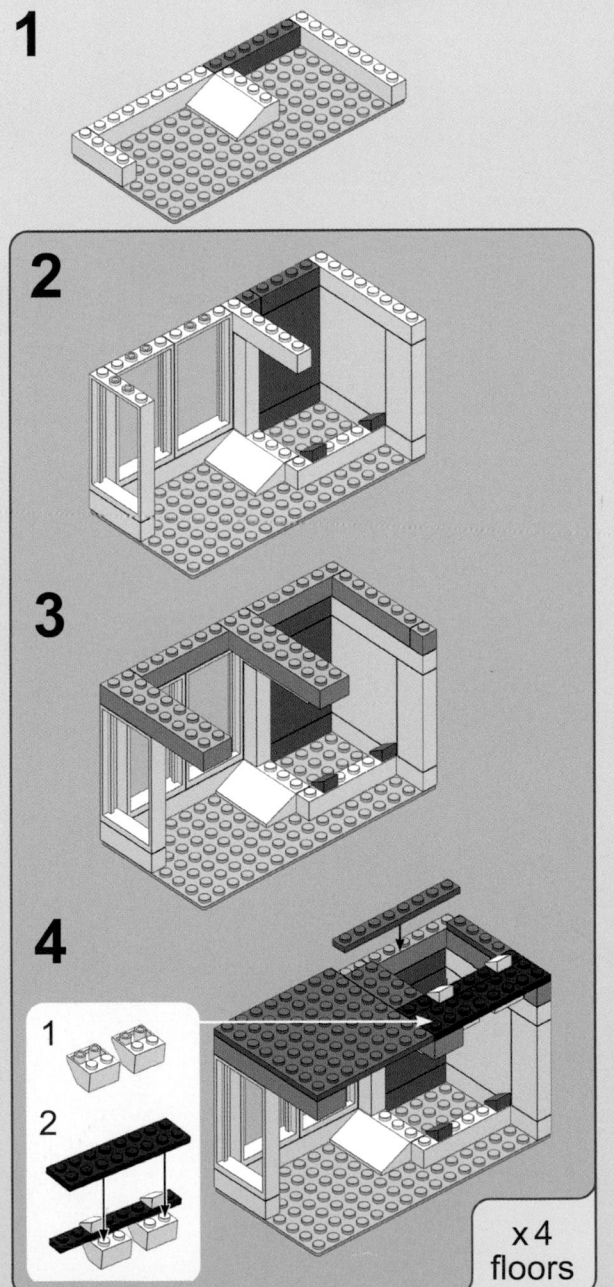

x4 floors

More than just buildings

Things to do and places to go make the city exciting!

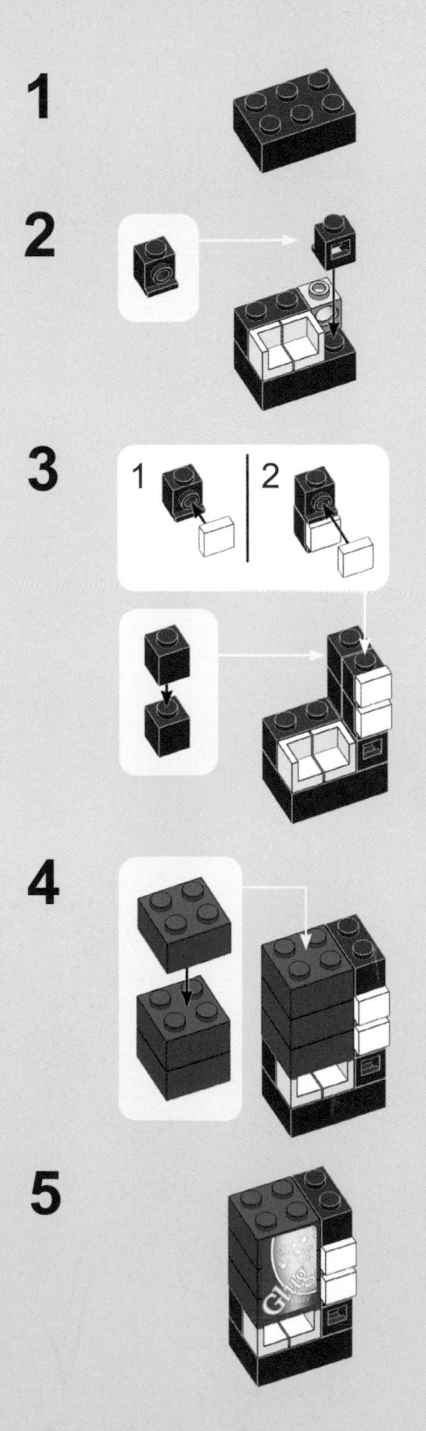

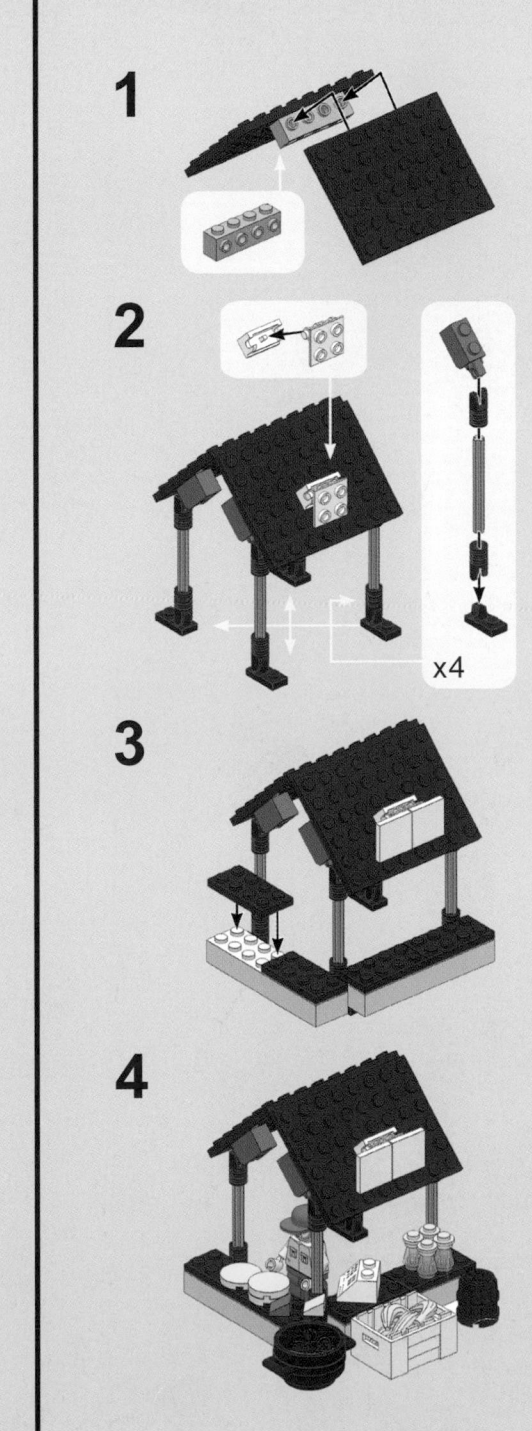

What else can you add to your city to bring it to life?